Ceolta Seisiúin na hÉireann
Irish Session Tunes

The Red Book

100 Irish Dance Tunes and Airs
Selected by Matt Cranitch

To access companion recorded accompaniments online, visit:
www.halleonard.com/mylibrary

Enter Code
7533-1577-3152-6133

ISBN 978-1-84938-248-9

Contact us:
Hal Leonard
7777 West Bluemound Road
Milwaukee, WI 53213
Email: info@halleonard.com

In Europe, contact:
Hal Leonard Europe Limited
42 Wigmore Street
Marylebone, London, W1U 2RN
Email: info@halleonardeurope.com

In Australia, contact:
Hal Leonard Australia Pty. Ltd.
4 Lentara Court
Cheltenham, Victoria, 3192 Australia
Email: info@halleonard.com.au

OSSIAN

Design by John Loesberg

Special thanks to Brian Denington of *Cuirluin Prints*,
for his permission to reproduce some of his
paintings of Irish musicians.
On this cover, left to right: Sonia O'Brien,
Gus Russell, Ellen Barker & Padraig O'Keeffe.
For more information see last page.

Other titles in this range of session tunes books are:

Irish Session Tunes, The Orange Book
by Bríd Cranitch, OMB 153   ISBN 1 900428 17 2
CD edition OMB84 ISBN 1-900428-77-6
Irish Session Tunes, The Green Book
by Geraldine Cotter, OMB 141 ISBN 1 900428 56 3
Irish Session Tunes, The Red Book
by Matt Cranitch, OMB 142   ISBN 1 900428 61 X

This collection contains a varied selection of tunes, some of which are popular and widely played, others not as well-known. The different dance rhythms – double jigs, slides, slip jigs, polkas, reels, hornpipes and set dances – are included, in addition to some airs. The number of tunes in each category represents, approximately, the relative popularity of the various types of tune, with the reel undoubtedly being the most popular.

Traditional music is subject to continuous change and variation as it is passed from one player to another, and so there is no one 'exact' version of any tune. Even if versions are very similar, they are never identical. Those given herein may be considered 'fiddle versions', in that they are well suited to this particular instrument. However, they are also suitable for the other instruments played in traditional music. In a small number of cases, it may be necessary to modify the tunes slightly so that the notes fall within the melodic range of some instruments.

Bainigí taithneam as an gceol seo – enjoy these tunes.

Matt Cranitch

TAKE A BOW (Ossian OSS CD 5) features thirty three tunes from this book, arranged and played by Matt Cranitch in fifteen contrasting selections. Additional instrumentation and accompaniment are provided on various tracks by Dave Hennessy (melodeon), Mick Daly (guitar), Eoin Ó Riabhaigh (uilleann pipes), Bríd Cranitch (piano and harpsichord), Colm Murphy (bodhrán), Tom Stephens (guitar).

GIVE IT SHTICK (Ossian OSSCD 6) contains a further representative selection of thirty tunes on fifteen tracks, again featuring the same musicians.

Index

DOUBLE JIGS

1. Tripping up the Stairs

2. Father O'Flynn

3. Connie O'Connell's Jig

4. The Frost is all over

5. The Eavesdropper

6.   The Geese in the Bog

7.   The Price of my Pig

8.   The Banks of Lough Gowna

9. The Lucky Penny

10. The Merry Old Woman

11. The Gullane Jig

12. The Humours of Lisheen

13. Up and About in the Morning

14. Petticoat Loose

15. Tell her I am

16. Munster Buttermilk

17. The Irish Giant

18. The Sporting Pitchfork

19. Brennan's Favourite

20. Willie Coleman's Jig

SLIDES

21. The Dingle Regatta

22. The Gleanntán Slide

23. Johnny Murphy's Slide

24. Michael Murphy's Slide

25. Danny Ab's Slide

26. Dan O'Keeffe's Slide

27. The Cúil Aodha Slide

28. Nell O'Sullivan's Slide

29. The Toormore Slide

30. Pádraig O'Keeffe's Slide

SLIP JIGS

31. Hardiman the Fiddler

32. Port an Deoraí

33. The Boys of Ballysodare

34. The Foxhunter's Jig

POLKAS

35. Maurice Manley's Polka

36. The Ballydesmond Polka

37. Din Tarrant's Polka (1)

38. Din Tarrant's Polka (2)

39. The New Roundabout

40. The Cappamore Polka

41. Matt Teehan's Polka

42. Dan Coakley's Polka

43. Pádraig O'Keeffe's Polka

44. The Blue Ribbon

45. Mick Duggan's Polka (1)

46. Mick Duggan's Polka (2)

47. Mick Duggan's Polka (3)

48. Farewell to Whiskey

49. The Knocknaboul Polka (1)

50. The Knocknaboul Polka (2)

REELS

51. The Providence Reel

52. The Wise Maid

53. The Sligo Maid

54. The Congress

55. Dinny O'Brien's Reel

56. Eileen O'Callaghan's Reel

57. The Pigeon on the Gate

58. The Killavil Reel

59. Far from Home

60. The Volunteer

61. The Boys of Malin

62. The High Road to Linton

63. The Monsignor's Blessing

64. The Wild Irishman

65. Andy McGann's Reel

66. The Humours of Scariff

67. The Maid behind the Bar

68. Paddy Ryan's Dream

69. The Crib of Perches

70. The Broken Pledge

71. Master Crowley

72. The Roscommon Reel

73. All Hands Around

74. The Bantry Lasses

75. O'Dowd's Favourite

76. Sean Reid's Reel

77. The Tullagh Reel

78. The New Policeman

79. Rattigan's Reel

80. The Bunch of Keys

81. Jenny's Welcome to Charlie

82. Lord Gordon

HORNPIPES

83. Pretty Maggie Morrissey

84. Fallon's Hornpipe

85. Ballymanus Fair

86. The Stack of Wheat

87. The Galway Hornpipe

88. Father Dollard's Hornpipe

89. Higgins' Hornpipe

90. Walsh's Hornpipe

91. Cross the Fence

SET DANCES

92. The Job of Journeywork

93. Madam Bonaparte

94. The Blackbird

95. Saint Patrick's Day

AIRS

96. An Buachaill Caol Dubh

97. Táimse im' Choladh

98. Na Connerys

99. A' Raibh Tú ag an gCarraig?

100. Pléaráca na Ruarcach

Two recordings with many of the tunes in this book,
played by Matt and friends are available:
Take a Bow: Ossian OSS CD 5
Give it Shtick: Ossian OSS CD 6

Ossian Publications produce a large range of Irish and
Scottish music for traditional & classical instruments as
well as collections of tunes, songs,
instruction books and items on the history of Irish Music.